In the Making of Goodbyes

poems

Carol Lynn Stevenson Grellas

Clare Songbirds Publishing House Poetry Series
ISBN 978-1-947653-35-1
Clare Songbirds Publishing House
In the Making of Goodbyes © 2018 Carol Lynn Stevenson Grellas

All Rights Reserved. Clare Songbirds Publishing House retains right to reprint.
Permission to reprint individual poems must be obtained from the author who owns the copyright.

cover art copyright © 2018 Clare Songbirds Publishing House
Printed in the United States of America

FIRST EDITION

Library of Congress Control Number 2018958414

Clare Songbirds Publishing House Mission Statement:
Clare Songbirds Publishing House was established to provide a print forum for the creation of limited edition, fine art from poets and writers, both established and emerging. We strive to reignite and continue a tradition of quality, accessible literary arts to the national and international community of writers, and readers. Poetry manuscripts are carefully chosen for their ability to propel the expansion of art and ideas in literary form. We provide an accessible way to promote the art of words in order to resonate with, and impact, readers not yet familiar with the siren song of poets and writers. Clare Songbirds Publishing House espouses a singular cultural development where poetry creates community and becomes commonplace in public places.

140 Cottage Street
Auburn, New York 13021
www.ClareSongbirdspub.com

Contents

Secrets
Concavities	9
Her Body Asleep beneath Your Feet	10
Birdsong	11
Exit	12
On Finding a Suicide Note	13
Diary Secrets from 1966	14
Prolonging Destiny: A Coward's Confession	17
Lavender Tea Euthanasia	18
One Year Follow-up	19
Violet Fields Forever	20
You, Me and Angry Birds	21
When You're Most Lost	22
The Earth is Flat	23
Instructions on Shortness of Breathing	24
In the Silence	25
Doors	26
In the Name of Mourning the Morning	27
Motherless	28
Says the Door Opening and Closing Shut	29
The Exhaustion of Relentless Caring	30
Turning the Car Around	32
Prayer for the Unborn	33
A Note to My Mother After Her Death	34
With Devotion for My Mother Ten Years After Her Death	35
The Implausible Life without You	36
Seeded	37
A Thousand Apologies	38
The Piano Bench	40
Being Nostalgic	41
Yes, I Want the Moon	42

Remembering
My Age in Poem Years	45
Confessions at Midnight	46
Immigrant Grounds	48
Learning to Count	49
Cipher Song	50
Into Little Pieces	51
Arousal in the Middle of Everything	52
Single-Cell	53
In the Frenzy of His Premature Departure	54

Beautiful Dead Girl Who Owns Infinity	55
On Remembering His Melancholy	56
In the Making of Goodbyes	57
Sunday Laments	58
To My Only Lover	59
Women at Fifty	60
Child Interrupted	61
Poet Song	62
Instructions from an On and Off Lover	63
Bleakest Dance of the Downhearted	64
Magic Man	65
Rambler	66
Take Me to the River	67
Aria	68
Raincheck Prayers	69
Untraceable	70
Blessing Eclipsed by Shadows	71

For my children

The most wasted of days is the one without laughter

~e.e. cummings

The author would like to thank the publications where the works have originally appeared.

"You and Me and Angry Birds," *Circa*
"A Thousand Apologies," *The Foliate Oak*
"Doors," *Curio*
"Instructions to My On and Off Lover," *Apeiron Review*
"In the Making of Goodbyes," *Wilderness House Review*
"Lavender Tea Euthanasia," *New Mirage Review*
"Violet Fields Forever," *New Mirage Review*
"Prolonging Destiny," *Dead Mule*
"One Year Follow up," *Triggerfish*
"On Remembering His Melancholy," *The Light Left Behind*
"Poet Song," *Tinfoil dresses*
"Rambler," *Eve Anthology Fortunate Child Press*
"Raincheck Prayers," *Umbrella Factory*
"To My Only Lover," *Eat a Peach*
"Take Me to the River," *Eve Anthology Fortunate Child Press*
"Seeded," *Pieren's Fountain*
"Aria," *Joyful!*
"The Earth is Flat," *Dogplotz*
"In the Silence," *Chantarelles's Notebook*
"The Piano Bench" *Poetry Quarterly*
"Sunday Laments," *The Blue Hour*
"Diary Secrets from 1966," *Burningwood*
"Bleakest Dance of the Downhearted," *The Knot Journal*
"Being Nostalgic," *Crack the Spine*
"Birdsong," *The Bookends Review*
"On Finding a Suicide Note," *The Same*
"Motherless," *Sheila-Na-Gig* pushcart prize nomination 2016
"The Exhaustion of Relentless Caring," *Sheila-Na-Gig*
"Turning the Car Around," *Sheila-Na-Gig*
"Prayer for the Unborn," *Sheila-Na-Gig*
"The Implausible Life Without You," *The Tower Poetry Journal*
"Immigrant Grounds," *Peacock Journal*
"Cipher Song," *Subliminal Interiors*
"Into Little Pieces," *Five Poetry*
"Single Cell," *The Grey Sparrow*
"Woman at Fifty," *Mothers Always Write*
"Instructions on Shortness of Breathing," and
    "Child Interrupted," *Touch the Journal of Healing*
"Untraceable," *The Olive Press*

Secrets

Concavities

With persistence of fingers on keys,
we are having an argument

my hands holding the accordion
between the breath of birds pulsing

through bellows. Today you are a melody
out of tune. I want to shove a reed

against your mouth and pray
you'll sing like a canary. But there's no

valve that offers an apology while both
hands are playing solo. If I cried

at the sign of leaking air, would it be
enough? Will you ever know the difference

between a squeezebox and a beautiful
bandoneon? Sometimes I sit on the edge

of our bed and pray for a righthand manual
but you are a buttonboard kind of man

a musician whose notes hover over rows
and rows of scales, oblivious to the arrangement

of melody, your perplexity a chromatic conundrum,
wings unfolded without flight, a disappointment

to any lover who might have hoped for song.

Her Body Asleep beneath Your Feet

In the dream, there's no room
for rain, or the sound of hands
          reaching through winds
     for lost birds.
There's only singing, if you listen
     long enough to forget.
    Death
was there before you knew
the meaning. In your mother's eyes
   there are tears on flowers
         and traces of perfume
from broken bottles. Water is always
collecting in her palms. Sometimes
       she scatters
her emptiness like the scent
    of gardenias in April.
She keeps her secrets
     dabbed behind each ear
and anywhere the darkness
sneaks in. You are between
           storms, waiting
waiting, waiting.
There is always a painting
better than your life, a story you'd rather
    become
  and you want to tell her, to bring her
with you, and it almost happens but she

never wakes up.

Birdsong

That on a day like any other,
I walked hand in hand with my mother
away from the rose garden where my father
stood with his hunting rifle pointed towards
the sky; a place of promises, paradise and stars
or unseen angels who watched over the meek
and the wicked and sometimes intervened
if wishes were granted, if enough Hail Marys
were said and if some saintly soul
long dead was watching out for you.

That on that day like any other I heard
my father break my mother's heart
with his threats of violence to himself
and anyone in close range, where I'd been
mesmerized by two robins who fed their young
as they flew back and forth from their nest
of twigs maybe a hundred times between them,
when my mother pulled me along the cobblestone
path into a grove of trees; our makeshift shelter
where bullets might weave in and out
of leaves and never find the mark or even
that mama bird whose beak was full of berries.

That on a day like any other, I walked hand
in hand with my mother, faster and faster
until we were long past the garden
far beyond the reach of my father
and his gun, when we heard a shot
then another, and I thought about those
baby birds waiting for their mother and how
in the middle of mayhem, they were unaware,
their necks outspread into the heavens,
mouths wide open, without a care.

Exit

To me, myself who cannot be me,
who will not share this incurable
sadness outside my compass
beyond my one and only one
whether or not there is another
to listen, to hear this cry for nothing,
this scream for everything, this need
for help that can't be heard, that has
no voice that won't be silenced
with fear, with all my years of broken
hearts from fragments cracked, little keys
still locked like living teeth but splintered
and filled then camouflaged with titanium
posts that bend like the core of another
and another due to circumstances,
unforeseen yet always present, never
near enough to examine, never far
enough to really be gone, only there
in the lambent light of morning
after it's too late, my body pressed
into itself, lost and unlost, found
and unfound by someone else—
my child, my mother, god…

On Finding a Suicide Note

You told yourself it was easier
to imagine a thousand reasons
why, than to know any one answer.
There was glory in the theory

of having no choice.

He was your hero, more
magical than Jesus or so you
thought. He smoked Winstons
and blew smoke rings in the air.

You thought he was invincible.

You were expecting a fairytale,
your head full of forget-me-nots.
You used to sit in his old Ford Woody
and he'd sing every song on the radio.

His pockets were stuffed with flowers

and a tiny bird he put in your hand.
It was a sparrow with a broken wing.
He taught you how to trust a wounded
thing, how to bring it back to life.

Diary Secrets from 1966

Jimmy was a dreamer,
a handsome James Dean kind of guy.
He decided at 17 he was in love,

so he eloped with his child bride
and kept it a secret until nobody
would question her age.

He loved his bride and she loved him.
They had a baby daughter
who was a dreamer too.

Jimmy had tiny flecks of gold in his eyes
that looked like the sun had burned right
through them.

Jimmy loved to dream but he loved
his child bride and daughter more
than any dreamer would think possible.

When he was 20, he was drafted
in the Korean War. He didn't like war
so he pretended he was blind and wore
a patch over his right eye

and when that didn't work he bought
a sunlamp and stared into the light
for 29 minutes a day.

Jimmy was never really blind in either eye
but his dreams began to be slightly blurred.
When the army said he could still see

well enough to kill a man, he went off to war.
Years went by and he sent love letters
home to his child bride and daughter

who were both growing up, alone.
Some of the letters spoke of things he missed
from back home. All of the letters had a pencil
sketch of wild horses running through a field.

When Jimmy returned from Korea, he was different.
He stayed out all night and played cards.
He drank a lot of whiskey, because
his dreams were more like nightmares.

He went to strip-clubs and bars, parading
around with streetwalkers, according
to his child bride. He started talking about

the men in his platoon. He wore a fedora
with a feather, wedged beneath a black satin ribbon.
Jimmy loved Winston cigarettes.

Sometimes he drew horses but they weren't running
free anymore. They looked sickly, their heads
hung down, their tails never flowed in the wind.

Jimmy's mother was concerned. She asked the doctor
to straighten him out. She ordered electric shock
therapy to get rid of his nightmares.

Jimmy told his daughter he was being followed.
He said people slipped things in his drinks.
He said he chewed bubblegum
to get rid of the taste.

He started hallucinating. His dreams were not
dreams anymore. Jimmy couldn't tell the difference
between his child bride and a streetwalker.

He acted funny, told his daughter not to look at his eyes.
Not to stare at the sun and never trust anyone, especially
men with fedoras who started hanging around after
hours, leaving ashes on the steps.

Jimmy liked to smoke but those ashes weren't his.
He began to fear for his life and his family's lives too.
He started locking doors and feeling paranoid.
He wrote crazy stories in a secret black binder.

One night, Jimmy took an overdose of sleeping pills.
His daughter found him with his eyes closed.
Jimmy didn't need a patch anymore.

When they buried him they draped his coffin
with an American flag. His daughter kept it
with his drawings of horses, the ones with their tails
whipping through the wind.

Years later someone told the family that Jimmy was in
a special troop the government called
Operation Midnight Climax.

He'd been part of an experiment that went
terribly wrong. Jimmy had been playing Black Jack
at a safe-house set up by the CIA.

Jimmy died an unsung hero. But his daughter never
doubted his dreams were real, even when they became
more like nightmares.

Some days she turns on the sunlamp for 29 minutes
and lets the warmth surround her face. She wears
a patch on both eyes to protect her from the light
or anything else she doesn't want to see.

She says Jimmy's dreams are alive in her.
She runs her fingers over his pencil sketches and reads
herself to sleep with the crazy stories he wrote
in the secret black binder.

She dreams of horses and unsung heroes
and all things that sound too impossible
to be true.

On his birthday every year she takes out
the folded American flag, drapes it over her bed,
puts on his feathered fedora and smokes
a Winston cigarette,

then chews one piece of bubblegum.
Because Jimmy would have liked that.

Prolonging Destiny: A Coward's Confession

You're unpacking boxes in a warm garage,
recovering treasures and mislaid years
all folded in cardboard and stacked

to the ceiling. Blocks of things now
fastened inside, like butterfly wings
pinned to canvas or once spoken words

from years ago, and you hear your mother
calling your name, and you hear your answer
through muffled walls, and you moan your prayer

to an unseeing Jesus as if forever can be repaired,
and you sense the slap of your father's hand,
and you hum that song that you always sang

when the world moved faster than the pace
of your heart and nothing mattered but a kiss
on the cheek or a sweet goodnight under a delta moon,

or the language of children when someone listened,
or the wedge of a peach into a milk-filled bowl,
or your grandmother's voice through a dovetailed

drawer, where you kept all the pictures of lifeless
people whom you've never stopped loving
yet still can't decide if they remember you now.

And just when you open the carton marked
"keepsakes" a black widow spider grazes
the box, and you grab a broom to smash

its belly, then shudder in shock while
the hourglass spurts right there on your memories,
you and infinity just one smack away.

Lavender Tea Euthanasia

If I live to be ninety-three, hair the color
of oyster shells, my body twisted like an arthritic
human braid, all beats used up from a pacemaker
driven heart, a onetime added, stop start device—

If I live to be ninety-three, clothes smelling
of cedar and smoke, cigarettes stored under
the sink beneath a worn-out rag and stain covered
book, where no burglar would think to look,

between the photos of two long dead sons,
a cancer-killed husband, sepia memories
of forgotten no-ones, with an Alzheimer
grin on my sunken face, unaware of names
or anyplace—

If I live to be ninety-three, bring me lavender
tea in a gilded cup, the woody scent wicking up
my nose; nostrils flaring like an opened rose
from the aroma of an herbal cure, with a morphine
dose to blur—

If I live to be ninety-three, simmer the flowers
to a boiling degree for my failing mind
while I lounge on a fainting couch. A killing
so kind, my murdering plea when I no longer
know, who's you or me.

One Year Follow-up

While we were waiting for your one year
follow-up, I was counting men in the room
without wives, I was thumbing through

articles of revamps for kitchens and broken
bedrooms in need of whistles and bells.
I was planning our meal of bacon wrapped

steaks with coconut rice and artichoke soup,
thinking how exhausted I was from a night
of no sleep. While we were waiting for your

one-year follow-up, I guesstimated odds
for a chance of good outcomes, how many
people were being given bad news, how many

came expecting answers, how many knew
how to interpret the eye roll or the implausible
quiet that punctuates fear.

Violet Fields Forever

Through the low hum of bees
she wanders the fields of lavender
beyond the high-stemmed rows,
past purple corollas of pinecone
flowers, in her tartan frock; pockets
full of unanswered prayers—

with ladybugs scattered over opened
blooms and the white froth of spittle
bugs attached to unsuspecting
leaves. Here you'll find her
immersed in the foliage, drunk
on the lilac aroma of earth's

fragrant garden, where no one can
see as she bends to her knees
in search of a wizard, the maestro
of maestros, with unrequited
wishes that dissolve in the wind
like the foam of an insect with preying
mouthparts that pierce unknowing ears.

You, Me and Angry Birds

I'd like to enable the giant eagle to bomb
the green pigs, spare the eggs until
our house is wiped clean of landmines—

remove all ticking clocks calculating
intentions of winning. I am already
weary from this game, the multiple levels

of infinity, how long this round will take to end.
In my dream you survive with strategy, solve
the puzzle of breaking through balloons

leading the flock. You shatter woodpiles, douse
endless fires and drink the flames for ammunition.
I can't outrun the finish, this sequence of inaccessibility.

I look to you for hope, for knowledge that someone
is mastering the intricacies of timing, the art
of resolving riddles. I can't find my way

through the grid. I've given up too soon,
turned off the sound, laid down my slingshot
praying for glory, while you unlock the stars.

When You're Most Lost

Remember how you curled yourself
deep in the womb of a mattress, the way
you once slept safe in the hollow
of your mother's belly, a little being
waiting to be born? Every miracle
is an act of God.

You wore light from the chandelier
like an angel's nimbus, your head held
high, arms raised for wings where no gale
or breeze could take you down. Pretend
you're a cloud; let the storm blow through you.

Layer petals from the rose of peace above
the lawn in garden soil and press your head
on the flower's corolla until you breathe
the newness of spring into your pores.
You are made of beauty and beauty
is made of you.

Lay down in mourning on graveyard grasses,
listen for beats of long buried hearts;
your ear pushed hard in the meadow's green veil.
Hear death that way, where no reply
is the answer. Heaven exists
in the easy pause of nothing.

The Earth is Flat

My toes hang over curled and bent
corkscrewed around the edge.

I waver towards the fall, peek below
and envision the length of infinity.

I wonder how it feels to be dead?

The August air is too thick to inhale,
one swallow holds back a stagnant heart—

I manage a breath, say her name,
push the spade deep in soil, unearth

eternity and I want to jump in.

Instructions on Shortness of Breathing

*The onset of relief and ease of breathing
should occur in minutes and will persist
for several hours.*

While you slumber through your velvet
dreams, no longer jaundiced, I'll slip within
imaginings, assist the wooziness and ease
the breathing, and if you rise before you wake
I will forgive you; the onset of relief.
Pray for me, for these will be tortuous days.

*There's no lessening this disease,
a rare degenerative disorder. The rate
of progression differs. Not every patient
experiences these symptoms.*

There's remission for your illness supplied
by hospice vials in amber shades. I've asked
politely for a pardon from the Sun, that you
might rest awhile before the moonlight comes
to bathe you in your satin sheets and ease
the grace of sleeping.
Pray for me, for these will be tortuous days.

*During the tube's placing, gagging may occur—
water is given while the patient swallows.
Great care must be taken to ensure
that it has not passed through the windpipe
and down into the lungs.*

I will rest gladiolas in a vase of water
by your bed. Great care will be given to
ensure ampoules are ready when the nurse
arrives to offer morphine, though I will not be
prepared for what may follow.
Pray for me, for these will be tortuous days.

In the Silence

I said it in the silence
when the air felt thin
when the light was low
and so was I.

I said it in the hour
when there was no need
when the breath was slow
and so was I.

I said it in the madness
when no one heard
when the chaos killed it
and so did I.

I said it to the window
when answers left
and glass stood between us
and so did I.

Doors

She fears the sound of snapping,
and the click of an opening when her hand
turns a knob; or the annual break of the wishbone
in a bird's tiny breast; this is the same

as the fork in the road, suspended
on the premise of what is and what is yet to be
the waiting of motion, a handle moving
further to the right, allowing light

through a keyhole's eye to hers. She's learned
to delay the last rotation, spinning the knob
counterclockwise then back suspended

between the threshold of the here and after
until her wrist becomes weary from indecision,
until she stands stagnant on the verge

of an entrance long enough to forget
anything on the other side.

In the Name of Mourning the Morning

In your final days, I lost track of who
I was, before the sun was full of night

as if there was no room for me without
the light of you to make my shadow.

There is only darkness now,
in all the mornings after.

The last time I sat with you, a breath
ricocheted between us, life and death

lost its way somewhere in the universe.
Wherever you are waiting, watching

from afar, please know, I did my best
to love you, to be a good daughter.

Motherless

Mother, nothing's quite the same
these days, and living is a harder thing to do
the way the roses cup the sun is so unbearable,
reminding me of you, as blossoms quiver
all unwoven grasping hummingbirds and bees,

the way your lip became a trembling flower,
the cry for morphine on your tongue
with sorrow as we'd count the hour,
unknowing all the quickness in a seraph's
step; their wings, a dance with grace,

but how I miss the comfort of your face.
Yours was not a selfish way to die,
our home your hospice as we each took turns
to lie beside you in your bed, like shepherds
guiding you to light, though one by one

we whispered, *do not go gentle into that good
night*. You, much braver than I'd ever known,
a warrior when illness stole your flesh
but left a hollow where a body used to sleep.
Sometimes I weep then wish I had a minute

more to say, your beauty was magnificent,
especially on your dying day. I think of you,
our midnight's last goodbye, remembering,
you said my name and then I watched you fly…

Says the Door Opening and Closing Shut

Once a child pretended that her dolls
could talk, she'd dress them in soft knitted
clothes, prop them on the windowsill
one after the next, wondering how many
it would take to fill a roomful of emptiness,
says the mirror across the wall.

Once a child kept a Bible by her bed
with handwritten notes to herself of things
she might forget someday and one letter
she found in her mother's room, saved
but never read, says the rosary in the drawer.

Once a child stared for hours at a plastic
globe hanging from the chandelier above
her head, where she imagined an invisible
world full of angels and dead people,
sort of like heaven but real, says the ceiling.

Once a child saved acorns in her pocket
from her trips to the cemetery on Sunday
afternoons until they overflowed and created
an endless loop from her house and back
that not even the wind could disrupt, says infinity.

The Exhaustion of Relentless Caring

When the mother says goodbye—
she is saying, I love you, look
both ways when you cross the street,
eat your peas and carrots, your name
is engraved in my eyes, you are all
I see, beware of strangers, there is
always a charming traitor
posing as your friend.

She is saying, tell me everything,
even things you're too afraid
to share, because she's grown
accustomed to worry, to hovering
over the kitchen sink, washing
the dishes and weeping.
She is saying, don't be stupid
for the sake of convenience,
follow the yellow brick road,
there's always a place called home.

When the mother says goodbye—
she is saying the world won't be gentle,
won't cradle you in its arms, won't
rock you to sleep without nightmares,
won't protect you from a nuclear war,
a certain apocalypse, water laced
with lead. She is saying bullets
are flying overhead or hidden
in the hands of madmen, and no
one will protect you from yourself.

She is saying all her nights
are spent in silent prayer, her days
calculating Christmases she has
left, presents still to wrap, gifts saved
for the future, decades from now,
even if she won't be there.

When the mother says goodbye—
she's making secret promises
to god, planning her good deeds
in exchange for karma, carving
your name on your skin, counting
up wishes and endless wondrous
things coming your way.

She is saying her life wasn't sacred
until you were born as she kneels
beside her bed to pray, humbled
by a greater power, she is saying
she didn't know joy until she saw
your face and she's grateful
for your life. She is saying
everything about you is just so
beautiful it almost breaks her heart.

Turning the Car Around

When I'm driving my car,
I still hear my dad's voice
say, *turn around sweetie, follow
that guy on the motorcycle,
he knows the way,* as if there was
some kind of grand payoff for
following a stranger in any direction
other than the one we were already
going. But that was his dementia
taking over and I knew better
than to listen to an old man whose head
was overrun with madness,
and by the time I could have
explained it to him, he'd long forgotten
he'd ever questioned which route to take
home or that there was another way
to anywhere, even here.
But now that he's gone I wish at least
once I'd done what he'd asked,
followed that guy on the motorcycle
as if that guy knew the way, that guy
with the wind at his back and his engine
revved up with the rebellious sun gleaming
down like a flare in the middle of the road
as we fumbled so desperately, as we tried
to navigate those last few months of his life
and the loss of his memories,
and all that we hoped to hang onto
like some kind of desperate salvation
or escape from reality, where the familiar
might keep us safe since neither of us
knew where the hell we were going.

Prayer for the Unborn

Maybe you can change it,
the way your mouth remembers
a kiss on the skin of an infant,
the petal soft curve of a cheek,
three drops of blood on the carpet,
the way your legs quivered and bowed,
lullabies echoing off mirrors,
hidden weeping save one stained
pillowcase, an incandescent candle
still lit near the statue of Mary,
an ache in the dark and the hope
of light between morning's
death of a fetus.

A Note to My Mother After Her Death

It's been chaos since you left
        but turmoil was always
            your alibi
    for an early departure. I've decided
love is harder to bear than grief
          if you need proof from
the other side.
            Sometimes I imagine you
      hanging
upside down from heaven, your hands
        probing through clouds,
    a thousand
angels gripping at your feet
              as you try
to seize anything below,
      even me.

With Devotion for My Mother Ten Years After Her Death

Because everything seems broken now, even words
and all memories are faded in a hollowed heart.

Because your picture doesn't remind me of you
anymore, as if there's no image really captured.

Because a dead sparrow makes me wonder if there are
no accidents and birds purposely fly into glass.

Because I've become obsessed with remembering
the sound of your voice until I actually hear it.

Because I've left your red overcoat hanging behind
my door as if you might one day walk in and need it.

Because I hear myself telling people I'm over your
death, crossing my fingers and wishing it were so.

Because every day I still read the note you left on
the nightstand a few weeks before you died

when you were overwhelmed with pain, yet still
managed to scribble, *this is a wonderful day.*

The Implausible Life without You

I've found you, mother, hidden in your childhood
ballet shoes, winding ribbons stained from wear,
the tips rubbed raw, frayed and peeled away
from the dance academy's hardwood floor. Beyond
every amen there is a door that leads me home again,
to you. All the nights I spend in dreams, your voice
echoes through imaginings like a sorrow in need of hope.
Even in death, there is no way to quell your weeping heart,
your spirit undone yet hampered by the weight of wings.

I've seen you, mother, passing through the light
rising overhead, inside a sleep that's never fully
realized, yet somehow wears me down enough
to hope that faith just might be real. I have a wreath
of flowers hanging above my head, the one I gave
to you, the one you said you'd always keep, half-broken
and frail from years of evenings holding in the dark.
There are lies in promises if one lives long enough
to prove a leap of faith might fail.

I've heard you, mother, calling my name on wintery
nights, your voice unwavering, your wraithlike shadow
young again, before your body was crushed
with disease. Listen, I want to tell you, you were
more than a mother to me, you were my truest friend,
your hands wrapped ever full of lavender and lilies
bending towards the nearest hallelujah. I remember
when I was small, the way you'd pin my hair with flowers
around my face, your fingers so controlled, pulling

back each tendril to its rightful place, as though
nothing would ever interrupt that kind of love.

Seeded

My fingers rim the lip's edge
of your favorite crystal, and I hear

the hum of hidden motion reverberate
about the room. I remember the clink

of sugar cubes dropping like noisy
tears, resting within a goblet

filled sphere of sparkling champagne.
How a thimbleful of bitters seeped

through undulant bubbly wine
and dissolved from whiteness

into nothing at all—only the sweetness
remains. That's how it is with you.

Even now as you visit me in dreams,
I stroke the outline of an unseen being

and hear the hymns of angels.
Today I saved small seeds removed

from the swollen calyx of dying
petunias. You are buried in the oldest

graveyard here. Your stone already
uneven from the movement

of ground. You've gone
too far from your own beginning

to ever be the same again.

A Thousand Apologies

After long days of tending to my mother's
needs, I would drive home from the house

where my parents raised me still
remembering the sound of music

that penetrated walls of bedrooms
in the earlier years where my brothers

and I slept night after night. The scent
of pancakes wafting through hallways

on Saturday mornings, the clanking
of tags from the family cat roaming

door to door until one of us opened
our bedroom cubical and whistled

a sharp but welcoming sign, signally
her to bolt for the nearest bed offered,

though mine was clearly the preferred
choice, if truth be told.

Those were the days of innocence
and laughter, when no one anticipated

concerns over tomorrows or yesterdays
nor secrets hidden between complicated

memories. Each of us closed off
to the other merely preoccupied

with the mysteries of adolescence
yet unaware we were in the midst of life

or some kind of strange pandemonium
called growing up.

How would I know there would be one
last drive when that house became quiet,

when my mother stopped breathing,
when no cat would pace that worn-out floor,

where no melody could be heard
through wallpapered walls

and the only fragrance noticed
was a lavender candle with its wavering flame

on my mother's bedside table.
How unprepared I was for the soundlessness

of leaving or that final ride back
from there to here while carrying a lifetime

of recollections with no reason to return.

The Piano Bench

I remember the way the bench felt
my legs bared against the upholstered
seat, my feet swinging wildly above

the floor, too small to reach the carpet,
all that joy between me and empty space,
the door kitty-corner and wide-open

to the garden's heat allowing a gentle
trace of ghostlike air inside the room—
her arm around me, I'd spoon

tight and feel the warmth of breasts
like a sheath from heaven around my bones.
I'd rest my fingers on that bench,

slip down to the hammered gold tacks and run
them lengthwise along the wood, as if there
was nothing misunderstood when music filled

my ears. Yet time would pass, she'd lose
her sons to tragedies, leaving us without
the men she'd birthed. We'd bury her;

unearth the ground beside our fathers' graves,
lower her deep inside someplace named eternity
vast as the difference between now and then.

Being Nostalgic

Through a keyhole, you'll find her room
quieted by a bed covered in silvered blue
lace, and a headboard carved with shells;
an arc of cherry wood that faces the northern
lights at night when the shade is drawn
up high enough to see the stars.

There's an old box housing a pair of palest
pink toe-shoes her mother once wore,
frayed at the point from a thousand pirouettes
a lifetime ago. In the mirror, over the door
a small heart with ribbons hangs above
the frame, the same one she used to wear

in her hair thirty years before. On the wall
are paintings of ballerinas, shadowed in black
and white, each one beneath glass
where the morning sun reflects its glare
as they stand in position, forever unaware
of the goings-on beyond a world of crinoline

and melodramatic art when no one could
tell the difference. A diary of her father's
rests atop the nightstand, yellowed and torn
from time and untold readings long after
his death. A favorite Winchester rifle

from his glory days of hunting leans kiddy
corner in the closet like an unseen belonging
as nothing feels as loved as it once
was in this room of forgotten things.
There are teacups, rings, snow globes,

crocheted blankets and autograph books
all from an era when signatures were
written from an ink jar, when nothing was
as hurried as it is now and she could still dial
the phone on the white wicker table and say,
this is your daughter calling, and someone

on the other end would whisper back,
I love you my darling girl, the only way
a mother or father is able.

Yes, I Want the Moon

Inside the hour of fireflies
God holds a lacewing above
a mist of stars. Do you want
the moon, Mary?

Insomnia weights my head
against the pillow. I have become
an island lost within the archipelago.
The morning fills my window

and glides along the sill. In time,
all things grow to one. Heat
permeates a glass-lit sun absorbing
light from outside in. Dying-time

is easier while you're here
with me. No one sees beneath
a row of tombstones where
nighthawks whip their feathered

limbs between unrequited prayers.
I don't hear the raindrops anymore
though they seep beneath my cover
from an open frame of sky, as souls

file through unending space, some
windowed place called Heaven. Within
a hollow womb the head will sleep
forever, but above the earth, the heart
is always waiting.

Remembering

My Age in Poem Years

This is the age of what needs to be done
rather than what's left not to do. The age
of nothing lost is better than something
gained. This is the age where I've buried
my parents and part of myself too. Where
I turn away from a mirror to remember
my youth. This is the age when I forget
about sleep yet dream about dreaming,
where I hold hands with God and forgive
the loveless for being unkind. This is the age
where I lose my rage and undo memories
that weigh down my soul, where I undraw
the line in the sand and offer my hand
to another. This is the age of desire
for a beautiful ending, firelight through
tears, answers given, unclaimed prayers
heard through the silence. This is the age
where I unfetter my children and revel
in their accomplishments and disregard
their failures. This is the age of holding
things in and leaving things out, this
is the age of sixty where I'm older
than this poem and everything
I'll ever write or hope to right
until the day, I die.

Confessions at Midnight

Since it isn't rape if you've asked
for it, if you've left your bosom
half exposed to light, the other
a hidden promise to come
or an invitation to an unwanted
admirer, your chest dabbed
with mineral oil and Shalimar.

Since everyone knows good girls
don't find mischief, and mischief
doesn't find them; love being
so complex and all, a moment
of passion easily confused
by at least one of the two parties,
especially the one who didn't hear,
no.

Since making a call to 911
isn't easy in the midst of
having your body pressed
against the cold glass table
he used to set his tumbler on
five minutes earlier, before
things got out of hand,
just after you'd offered him
a cocktail.

Since pretending nothing
happened made it go away
for the first few years, until
the night you gazed beyond
your window hoping to see
the Moon's face but, instead
you saw a lie in the Moon's place,
like an arrogant intruder in the dark.

Since you're older now and have
daughters of your own, and you need
to break your silence, let them know
once you were vulnerable, once
your fury was hushed by fear,
fear of judgment by the ones you loved

and especially the ones you didn't,
fear you'd be unbeautiful, undone
and you realize how much was taken
from you so long ago, on a night
you'd hoped forgotten and a memory
you'd wished erased.

So, you picked up the phone and dialed RAINN.
(Rape Abuse and Incest National Network)

Since the woman that answered
the phone sounded a little bit
like your mother and you almost
hung up ashamed to give your name,
and part of you wished she was
your mother, encouraging you to do
the right thing and then you said,

"I want to report a rape that happened
40 years ago," and you felt the light
of the Moon pierce through the darkness
like some kind of otherworldly intrusion
of truth: sweet as your mother's
kiss soft against your face just as
you remembered it, even though
she's been dead for over a decade.

So, you hung up the phone and wept
a little, not for the telling,
but for the not telling, the years
of keeping it between you and God,
tucked inside your heart's pocket
of old stories never shared.
And then you wept for all the years
of being ashamed, about something
so heinous… that was never your fault.

Immigrant Grounds

Let's pretend this isn't real;
that you and I never fought
and the silence between us

is a fixable truce. Let's be filled
with lengthy hallelujahs; both of us
giving in to the tangle

of memories years long past
that inflated our egos inch

by inch until we popped
from our own pomposity.

You were always beautiful
in the midst of an argument;
tears cleared with hard working

lashes, your nakedness exposed.
Let's pretend this was our only crime
while we stride together towards

immigrant grounds, a sacrosanct
place of newfound forgiveness,
my path yours, your path mine.

Our Elephant Walk to the burial
grounds of inevitable death,
one as sure as the other.

Learning to Count

First, there was one prayer,
    a way to say goodnight
the need to believe someone
    was watching
  over me.
First, there was one mother
    who said, 'I love you'
and that was enough to keep
      the monsters away.

First, there was the need
      to feel needed
and everything
    else seemed unimportant.
First, there was one father
    who said, 'don't worry'
as though two words could
      solve a whole lifetime
        of troubles.
First, there was one dance
        that broke through
  silence, boundless joy
    that made all things seem possible.
        First, there was one death
    and then,

there was another.

Cipher Song

How will I tell them I hear you singing?
You, the whisperer of abandoned hours
sending your music through soft magnolias
orchids embracing lost notes in the wind.

And here I am so deep in the thicket
down by the river of childhood dreams.
I'm wearing the moon-dress of starry array
barefoot in cattails that thirst for the Sun.

Come, I say, *sit here beside me*, we are
aligned now, disciple of death. Yours is the song
the loping deer follow, romping through
meadows where mustard seeds grow.

Yours is the voice the hobo cries
searching for memories lost in the years.
Yet how do I tell them I hear you singing—
this song that aches, this hyacinth's hymn?

So here I am, your twilight wanderer
seeking the solace of haunting sighs,
hands holding sorrows all tucked within pockets,
cheeks air-kissed by a blanket of leaves.

Once I held a nest in my palm where no
bird knew the warmth of a mother. Once
I held a bird in my palm where no mother
knew the warmth of a nest.

Yet here in the darkness I hear your singing—
a distant cantata that beckons me near.

Into Little Pieces

When she is small, her body bends,
an origami paper bird, halved and halved,
edges creased to perfect folds until
she lives within a pair of lungs, where
the flush of dawn never pierces the night-
tucked chill or another unpredictable
morning entering her windowsill.

When she is small, she dwells in a jingling
world of iridescent things with a pointillism
kind of view where the twinkling of tinsel
twists like licorice rope, an almost happy place
but without the sweetness and flavor of hope.

When she is small, she hears the heckle
of low-flying bees looming near
the magnolias trees; she remembers the sting
on unprotected skin of the little girl
who roved fields through marigolds and winding
roads, shadowed by someone else's load.

Arousal in the Middle of Everything

We, who found the trunk beneath the bed,
filled with imaginings of long ago children who
swallowed the wind and slept with a gale inside—

who slumbered to the sound
of clocks, to the thought of each new
day and a window's opening through emptiness—

who lost ourselves in the shadow
of another, or heard the cowbell
yet never bothered to remove the device—

who slid our bodies into the ravine
and forgot to touch the sunlight, asleep
to the droppings of leaves and the noise
    of God—

who sat on our mother's hope
chest and never noticed all the heartache
collected beneath...

who never apologized to ourselves
without regret, who hid our dreams
in a moonless sky,

shall, rise, *rise and always, rise.*

Single-Cell

One day, in a fidget of time
while limbs reached end to end
through a catacomb sky, a child

longed for the mother and father
as if the hierarchy could render
him back from whence he came.

Misplaced among the wooded forest
where boughs locked their tangled
limbs diagramed against the rainy

canvas of unparalleled proportion,
his head pressed until bones barked
skinless; he grew through the outer layer

of a tree as the womb that birthed him—
no longer in search of spring's
raiment nor tertiary wings, the boy

wept while decay of humaneness
turned to mulch and a firefly
lit the night to a daunting, umber glow.

In the Frenzy of His Premature Departure

I still hear an echoing
through my head,
one wife weeping
prayers being read,
children screaming
his name past the early hours
until they are mute,
their throats full of stars.

Beautiful Dead Girl Who Owns Infinity

And this is how I remember you
when I brush my hair, your fingers
dead in the coffin, mine still
warm but for the time I have left.

You, unmoving though the wind
races through your golden ashes
scattered among the pearly dogwood
and the few of us who wait for your soul

to lessen our journey with a godly sign
fragments of heaven scattered about
as you must be the glorious sun
in the afternoon or the long-eared

jackrabbit darting in and out of junipers.
Forgive me for being so needy,
for this pathetic cry that remains
unanswered, but I have scoured

the holiest of graveyards, bruised my feet
on uneven pavement, my endless excursion,
this hopeless expedition, for the tiniest
glimpse of you. Somewhere in the midst

of rage and sorrow hope awaits
like a morning feast yet always ends
with shotgun to the belly, no angels
in sight, one black crow circling overhead.

On Remembering His Melancholy

He was a rover with his hands, a brilliant fool
in need of a challenge, but I was only asking
for romance and a windy breath to ride away

on. We were strapped within ourselves, over
polished with manners, heavy with expectations.
It's hard to recall the way he held me

too careful for passion, no caress worthy
of lament, yet I can't forget his brother's
death and the nights we cried inside my bedroom

when even the softest touch gave way
to an open brokenness. A dying took
place in his eyes, and I wanted to hold him

with the kind of courage it takes to heal
that kind of sorrow, though it was more
than I could bear. Unmeasured grief wept

through his skin, my body doused with tears,
aching and weighted with loss, then failure for trying
to absorb that kind of mourning.

In the Making of Goodbyes

I'd like to send a prayer with the litany
of reasons my heart was broken
knowing you slept better the closer
you came to death. How you never

woke once to ask if there was anything
left unsaid. I can only think that dying
must be easier through the selfishness
of letting go. I've packed your things

in bags *return to sender* but kept them
all instead, I've hung your coats in darkness
near my Sunday best, with the rest
of what you'd call a tasteful array

of outerwear. Most days I rush
to find the warmth inside my closet—
a hurried guess of pulling something
from a room of memories suspended

on a wire. Today I feel a shiver through
the dimness, the faintest scent of you
wafting past my face; the air's familiar
trace, one hallowed moment in the midst

of leaving. Still, you never said goodbye.

Sunday Laments

There are days I think about the way we used to be together—
not so long ago when more than once, you said you loved me.
I still remember how that felt. I knew those words would vanish
the way a photograph fades after decades of growing old, the
way a memory is never right, the way a memory is never wrong.

But the hardest thing to remember is how my mother looked the
day she died, her chin trembling each time she'd take a breath. I
called the nurse to come over to help me bathe her in lavender
oil, her body soft as prayers. I used to tell people I wanted to be
a nurse dressed in all white, eyes full of hope and prayers. I can't
forget the way she held my hand and said, "It won't be long
now."

I asked if my mother could hear my voice. "No," said the nurse,
then sponged my mother's skin. But when we were done, she
pulled me near and whispered, "I was wrong, but I've never seen
anyone weep while comatose before," one tear rolling down my
mother's cheek.

I wept when she said that, and that nurse wept too. There are
days I think about the way we used to be together, your smile
forgiving, eyes full of all the people you'd loved and lost along
the way. Some days I could see beyond you and me, I could see
all the dreams you'd given up on, buried beneath your skin.

If I'd been a nurse, maybe I could have saved you a little
bit at a time. Maybe I could have saved us if I'd realized
the end was coming and maybe I could have warned you,
"It won't be long now." I could have whispered in your ear.
I could have said, I was wrong too, and maybe I would have

penetrated some of the brokenness from all those people who
hardened your heart, one let-down at a time. "Here's a
picture," I'd say in my dreams, "here's a memory of how we
used to look as children." And maybe you'd gaze up with a
trembling voice and mumble how you loved me again, both of
us weeping...

I'd be dressed in white, the scent of lavender on my hands.

To My Only Lover

Writer who molds lost clouds
into tiny poems across the sky
above windswept seeds disseminating
throughout the meadow, soon to be full

with flowers in the coming spring.
Writer, I love you, I am yours
for the asking, my limbs unfolded
my heart a song of flutes and strings

beautiful as an eight-voice choir
one mellotronic happening, exposed
as the ripest pomegranate hanging
from a blossoming tree, pick me!

I am certain you'll be pleased, there's
an ease about knowing you're listening
out there, somewhere, contemplating
our rendezvous, our soon to be midnight

climax; where are you?

Women at Fifty

When women at fifty lay flat
on their bellies, some will remember
the roundness that thrived

in the womb of their skin
where a fetus once swam;
now-hollowed figures where secrets

began and grew to a marvel beyond
heaven and stars. They'll turn
to their side without need

to surrender to the unwieldy
bundle that pushed against bones
and stirred through the twilight;

a disquieted wonder until slumber
was lost to the waking of being.
From a steeple of hope through

a spindrift of prayers they'll barely
recall a day without worry,
how they worshipped beginnings

then bellowed goodbyes.

Child Interrupted

I can almost see your face through
the tiny swell in my belly, still

there where you grew sweet like sugar
leaves in the fattened pulp of your human

incubator. Where I recited prayers
to freckled skin with no response

save the undulation of an occasional
flutter as if your answer came in the form

of hiccups or tiny spasms granting
reply beneath pulled flesh, until

your accidental fruition, when you arrived
with no warning; an embryonic

treasure that cut a swath through my
heart as you found your way to glory

the day you were nearly born.

Poet Song

You are the sleep that finds the night
and all of night that lifts the day, you are

the way from here to there, with love
inside a Sunday prayer. You are the book

all ribbon-wrapped with whispered psalms
heard everywhere, beneath the tiny maidenhair.

You are the parsley growing free,
you are lost then found in me, soft as wingtips

brush the sea. You are the shades of daffodils
with trumpets flared on golden hills—

you are the blooms on windowsills
and porches trimmed with sconces hung

with clappers chiming one by one—
you are the doorways in and out,

a hundred poems to write about, uncountable
trees in camphor green with fireflies glowing

in aubergine. You are the labyrinth of hide
and seek, you are my only winning streak—

you are the sparkling crystal bowl
that holds a sip to cleanse my soul.

Instructions from an On and Off Lover

Sing to me your quixotic song—
the kind caged birds will understand
like the dark-green voice of the olive tree

signaling wind when every leaf hangs
exhausted from last night's storm.
Ignore all wounds inside my wrists;

tattooed souvenirs from the first time
my spirit gave-way to weakness
in a lifetime too long to endure without

you. Never do anything sudden. The relief
of predictably, no matter how disastrous
is something I've grown accustomed to.

An unexpected good ending would surely
be the death of me. Even now, the thought
of happiness is almost unbearable,

like the smallest wing barely opening
to gusts of air from yesterday's flurry.
And when I feel unbeautiful, adore me

anyway with impossible devotion, made
more precious by your constant threat
of leaving. When it's over, tell me you need

a cigarette, pause by the door with a half-smile.
Ask that I bring your jacket over. After
you've gone, place your hand in the right pocket,

where you'll find your tobacco rolled with a small
handwritten note; my litany of reasons why you've left.
And when you light the tip, draw in the smoke

as words burns like tinder on your tongue;
just enough to keep you from turning
back, while I listen for your footsteps through

the tangle of bare branches again
and again and again.

Bleakest Dance of the Downhearted

When I dream of fire, I dream of you—
my lungs inhaling a red flamed fever
until the burn overcomes my being
or maybe it's just the end of world...

but only in that dream and yet there is
a suspension of life in sleep and I fear
death might arrive without warning, without
my need to panic or even my craving

to say goodbye. There is no allure in wandering
away to something strange, some far-off
place of loneness, since loneness isn't
about being alone. My mother always said

it is better to be wanted than to want, yet
you have become my outstretched desire,
my obsession for never leaving. If going
forward means a field of blackness without

you, where no lighted path will rinse my eyes
with your crimson haze of rapture, I will lay
myself down upon a pitch of smoldering
greenery, somewhere amid winter and spring,

my body exhausted, my heart still ablaze.
It is only in the windiest of hours that I have clung
to the sound of your voice echoed deep within
my ears, though I am terrified of the day

I will no longer hear you.

Magic Man
After reading Walt Whitman

You are the lilac sprig, the tang
of grass in spring, the sound
of trumpeters with high-knees
marching towards the sun—

I come to you with sumptuous
breath, eternal as the breadth
of cosmic stars. I'll linger here,
my dulcet mystic, midnight-soul

with promise. To deathless laughter,
the joy of babble and blush of orange
poppies bowed in open fields, you
are my buoyed hope, O flickering

love. Sweet leaves that rustle
to summer winds, chimes that ring
the clapper's bell, my lyrist
in the garden, where I hear

the tears of ghosts and songs
for saints in winter. Through the din
of chaos beauty comes. This is my
poem for you, my dedication

of unstoppable affection, endless
ardor, vast as infinity, sure as the rifle
firing and the heart exploding
from too much love.

Rambler

Here you are again, haunting my
midnight hours like a lonely pilgrim,
homeless amidst the stars. Long ago
your feet touched grass and we danced

barefoot through a pasture of zinnias.
Those were the days of fairytales:
bed-skirts made of eyelet-lace
and pillows holding fragile necks

for our mother's porcelain dolls.
There's no compartment large enough
to carry all my memories—and so
I shut this dovetailed drawer, your

letters crowding envelopes torn
against the slats. Sometimes I see
your linen dress blowing through
the clouds; you, riding on a filigree

horse, naked against the Moon. You've
broken free old friend, maneuvered
past the roundabout. Your flutelike song
a windy echo in all your deathless glory.

Take Me to the River

When muscles become limp
and knees almost unbendable—

when words are mostly wasted
and the aid of another is essential—

I will miss the clang of wind
chimes that dangle from magnolias

that rattle through the mist of rain.
Take me to the river where

the water meets the heavens, where
a thousand mallards wear emerald

wings and iron wetness into glass.
Sound the trumpeters who'll play

to rhythms of the wind, where
I will find my final rest upon

a bed of lilies. Lead me from the
bleakness into beautiful, once again.

Aria

Through the unblinking eyes of heaven
and the curled tongue of windswept clouds
we'll bend to death as soft as the daffodil.

Each to each, we'll bow upon the field
until our soil weeps with pale tears,
like stains on silk as the sound of carillons ring.

This, our assignation in a land of hymn-less
angels who only know of sanctity
through the blessedness of touching—

who will only hear singing when their ears
have finally deafened when the glorious
memory of home will forever be restored.

Raincheck Prayers

Thank you, Jesus, for 409 with its bleach-
scented lime. When my blind dog soils
the floor, the way it masks the stench of urine
is almost sacred. Just don't open the door—
the image of being that feeble will surely
do you in.

Thank you, Jesus, for my robe wrapped
tight, the morning's light and the hope
that it will be years before I need
a caregiver. I'm planning to lose my mind
before I know the difference.

Thank you, Jesus, for ten steps to the pot
of coffee, grounds perfumed with a hundred
years of mocha java blend, hands scooping
sunrise-medicine, too early for dirty martinis,
and the urge to say "frankly I don't give a damn."

Thank you, Jesus, for a thimbleful of jam
in its strawberry redness on toast before it seems
morose with its buttery spread holder, colder
than cold inside a two-piece glass-like coffin
for a tub of lard; better off dead, enough said.
Elvis has left the building.

Thank you, Jesus, for the feeding of fish
I gave my daughter, dropping pellets through
sullied water as Beta bubble their way to bliss
through mercurochrome seaweed; I take
my hormones; two a day, never miss.

Thank you, Jesus, for a list of tasks as I remove
my husband's hat tossed on the bed in haphazard style
remembering some cock and bull story
about fedoras and bad luck and who knows what
but, your guess is never as good as mine.

Thank you, Jesus, for each hour's time—
how that unseeing creature is howling
from the far-off room to mine as I say
these prayers and muster up the strength to mop
up another round of urine, no good deed
goes unpunished, amen.

Untraceable

The old willow where we'd kneel beside
the sunlit creek in search of tadpoles;
uncatchable as dreams.

The dreams of finches in an unlocked cage
perched above seeds while I'm trying
to hold them in my sleep.

The sleep as deep as the stupor
of a newborn after feeding
from an overflowing breast.

The very breast that held me close
enough to hear the heart of everything,
especially my own mother.

My mother forever stilled in photographs.
in an abandoned camera, broken but
alive inside.

The inside of a mirror, the way the reflection
echoes an image, boundless yet
lost to glass.

The glass he held before he downed
his last concoction of pills, one hand
embracing water, the other death.

Death that defies the eavesdroppers long
enough to miss the hooves of deer
and shallow fracas of those who never

heard it coming.

Blessing Eclipsed by Shadows

Now, as courage fades like the scent
of tuberose on even the softest skin—

now, as you look in the mirror and see
your mother's face instead of your own—

now, as each new day has become
camouflaged by that which is not
easily perceived—

now, as time has stolen the wonder
from all that once was mesmerizing—

now, as the day's weight guides you
through its addictions and careless routine—

now, as death has folded your arms
and buried its haste in suspicion—

now, as you gather your children only
to free them like horses that charge the gale—

now, that somehow, you've survived the chaos
arrived at this place, your fingers still counting
Hail Marys—

let the dawn embrace you, hold your hand
in warmth like a new beginning, your body

consoled, your heart gladdened
as you will walk easily, surrounded in light.

Carol Lynn Stevenson Grellas lives in the Sierra Foothills. She studied at Santa Clara University, where she was an English major. She is an eight-time Pushcart nominee, a five-time Best of the Net nominee and the winner of the Red Ochre Chapbook Contest, with her manuscript, *Before I Go to Sleep*. She is the author of two full-length collections of poetry, *Epistemology of an Odd Girl* (March Street Press) and *Hasty Notes in No Particular Order (*Aldrich Press) along with several chapbooks including her latest, *Things I Can't Remember to Forget* (Prolific Press). Her poems have been published widely in journals as well as anthologies. She is the poetry editor for *The Orchards Poetry Journal* and a member of Saratoga's Authors' Hall of Fame. According to family lore, she is a direct descendant of Robert Louis Stevenson, or at least her mother said so...

www.ingramcontent.com/pod-product-compliance
Lightning Source LLC
Chambersburg PA
CBHW062040120526
44592CB00035B/1709